SCIENCE **DISCOVERY** TIMELINES

KEY DISCOVERIES IN
EARTH
AND SPACE
SCiENCE

CHRISTINE **ZUCHORA-WALSKE**

LERNER PUBLICATIONS ◆ MINNEAPOLIS

TO MY SON TONY, PLANET PLUTO'S MOST ENTHUSIASTIC DEFENDER

cover image
Planet Earth in 1996, from the space shuttle *Endeavour*. The US space shuttle program began in 1981 and ran for thirty years.

Content consultant: Kevin Finerghty, Adjunct Professor of Geology, State University of New York at Oswego

Lerner Publications Company
A division of Lerner Publishing Group, Inc.
241 First Avenue North
Minneapolis, MN 55401 USA

For reading levels and more information, look up this title at www.lernerbooks.com.

Main body text set in Diverda Serif Com Light 11/14. Typeface provided by Linotype AG.

Library of Congress Cataloging-in-Publication Data

Zuchora-Walske, Christine, author.
    Key discoveries in Earth and space science / by Christine Zuchora-Walske.
        pages cm.— (Science discovery timelines)
    Audience: Ages 11–14
    Includes bibliographical references and index.
    ISBN 978-1-4677-5787-4 (lib. bdg. : alk. paper) — ISBN 978-1-4677-6157-4 (pbk.) — ISBN 978-1-4677-6248-9 (EB pdf)
    1. Discoveries in science—History—Juvenile literature. 2. Space sciences—History—Juvenile literature. 3. Earth sciences—History—Juvenile literature. 4. Astronomy—History—Juvenile literature. I. Title.
    Q180.55.D57Z83 2015
    509—dc23   2014026722

Manufactured in the United States of America
2 — DP — 9/1/15

CONTENTS

INTRODUCTION

Earth and space science are two very different things, but the two are intricately intertwined. Earth science is the study of the planet where we live and all its parts. These parts are Earth's atmosphere, land, water, and interior. Space science is the study of the universe through which Earth moves.

Together, Earth and space science have six main branches. Geologists study Earth's solid material and the processes that create Earth's structure. Meteorologists study short-term weather patterns to understand how weather affects human activity and Earth. Climatologists study long-term weather patterns to understand the reasons and the ways in which our climate changes. Oceanographers study everything—both living and nonliving—in Earth's ocean environments. Environmental scientists study how humans affect their environment. Space scientists study outer space and objects outside Earth and its atmosphere. Astronomers are one kind of space scientist. They use telescopes to see far into space. Aerospace engineers are also space scientists. They design satellites and spacecraft that gather information about distant reaches of the universe.

The history of Earth and space science is a story of change. For many thousands of years, humans believed that Earth and the heavens always were and always would be the same. They believed that humans were firmly planted on an unmoving, unchanging Earth that was at the center of the universe and that they would never venture beyond it. But in just a few centuries, these beliefs transformed dramatically. People invented tools, such as telescopes, that allowed them to see faraway objects. Scientists found evidence that Earth is not the center of the universe but is in a continual state of motion and change. They developed a better understanding of the natural laws that govern the motion of all objects. And humans used this understanding to send both people and instruments beyond Earth.

A series of timelines is one good way to tell the complex story of Earth and space science. Each timeline shows how scientists are linked in their efforts to better understand Earth and the universe.

The Grand Canyon shows how Earth's surface changes gradually over time. This image, taken from the International Space Station, was made possible by advancements in space science that made space travel a reality.

A Line That Shows a Story

A timeline is a visual representation of history. It displays a series of events and the dates on which they happened along either a vertical or horizontal line. These events are related to a common theme or period of time and are listed chronologically. That means they are arranged in the order in which they occurred.

Timelines tell a story by placing key moments in a logical sequence. They also help people understand the cause-and-effect relationship among events. In some cases, timelines span hundreds of thousands of years. In others, they cover a period of just a few hours or even minutes. Artwork often accompanies the entries in a timeline. Dates that occurred before a certain point in history frequently include the abbreviation *BCE*, which stands for "Before the Common Era." The Common Era is the period that began with the start of Christianity, or the birth of Jesus Christ.

Each chapter in this book begins with a timeline and then moves to a written story. You can read it in the way that helps you understand it best. Look at the visual highlights first and then read the details. Or start with the text and go back to check out the timelines.

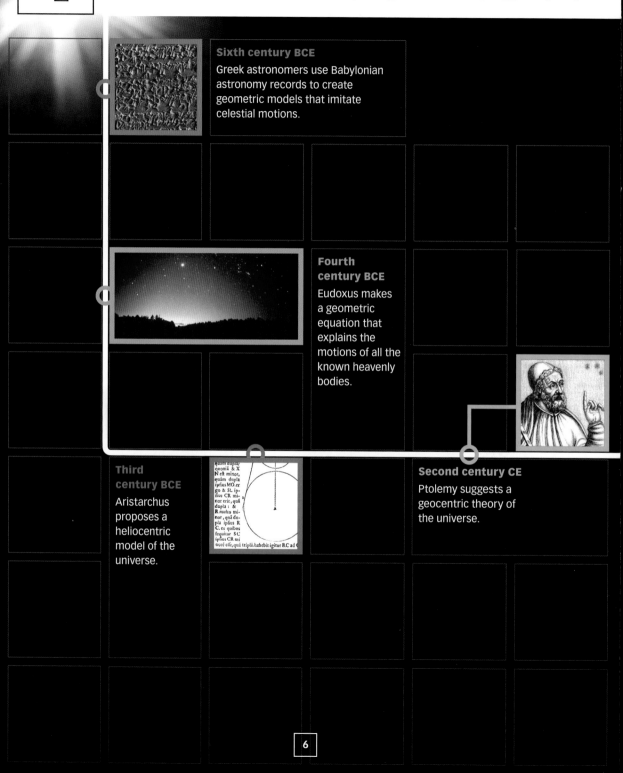

Sixth century BCE
Greek astronomers use Babylonian astronomy records to create geometric models that imitate celestial motions.

Fourth century BCE
Eudoxus makes a geometric equation that explains the motions of all the known heavenly bodies.

Third century BCE
Aristarchus proposes a heliocentric model of the universe.

Second century CE
Ptolemy suggests a geocentric theory of the universe.

COSMOLOGY

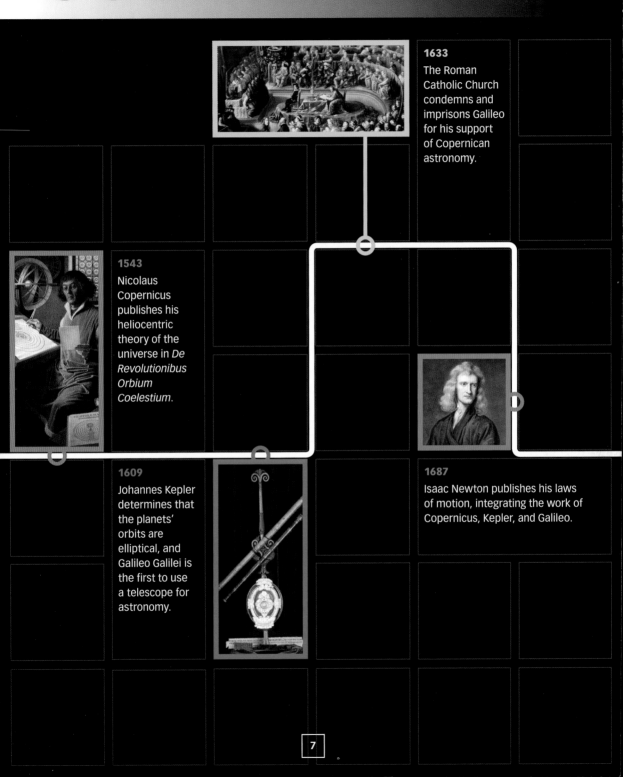

1633

The Roman Catholic Church condemns and imprisons Galileo for his support of Copernican astronomy.

1543

Nicolaus Copernicus publishes his heliocentric theory of the universe in *De Revolutionibus Orbium Coelestium*.

1609

Johannes Kepler determines that the planets' orbits are elliptical, and Galileo Galilei is the first to use a telescope for astronomy.

1687

Isaac Newton publishes his laws of motion, integrating the work of Copernicus, Kepler, and Galileo.

Where is the center of the universe? That question may seem ridiculous to people in the twenty-first century. Modern scientists believe that the universe has no center. The question seemed ridiculous to ancient peoples too but for an entirely different reason: the answer was so obvious.

That's because most people believed Earth lay motionless at the center of the universe. Their cosmology, or view of the structure of the universe, was geocentric. *Geocentric* means "Earth-centered." People had many good reasons for this belief. For starters, anyone could walk outside and see evidence to support it. Earth certainly didn't seem to be moving. But the heavens sure did. The sun crossed the sky every day. The moon and the stars crossed the sky by night. All of it, people presumed, must be moving around Earth. It took many centuries and a lot of evidence to change this view.

ANCIENT **ASTRONOMY**

Ancient peoples studied the sky closely. They noticed that the movements of the sun, the moon, and the stars followed regular patterns. These patterns helped people measure passing time. Patterns also helped them note when important events occurred during the year. And for many ancient peoples, the motions of celestial bodies happened because of divine forces. They believed that gods and goddesses controlled the heavens, which, in turn, affected human events.

Babylonians used tablets to track the movements of stars, Earth's moon, the sun, and other planets. This tablet is a record of the risings and settings of the planet Venus.

The Babylonians kept detailed records of the locations and motions of the stars, Earth's moon, and the sun. They also noted celestial events, such as eclipses. They used these records to create horoscopes, or diagrams that supposedly predicted events in human lives. The city-state of Babylon was part of the ancient land of Mesopotamia (modern Iraq). Babylonian astronomical records date all the way back to about 800 BCE. They continued until about 60 BCE.

Ancient scholars saw celestial bodies very much like what we see in modern times. But before telescopes, they couldn't see differences betweeen planets and stars.

Thanks to the Babylonians' plentiful and detailed records, their neighbors across the Mediterranean Sea, the ancient Greeks, had plenty of data to use in their studies of the universe. The Greeks also made astronomical observations to add to the data.

Greek astronomers wanted to create geometric models that explained celestial motions. This began in the sixth century BCE, with the Greek mathematician Pythagoras and his followers. Pythagoras believed that everything had a mathematical pattern or cycle. He thought that through mathematics, people could predict and measure natural events. He also believed that all heavenly bodies were spherical and moved in circles in space.

In the fourth century BCE, Greek scholar Eudoxus was the first to form a general geometric equation that explained the motions of all the known heavenly bodies. He, like most other ancient Greek scholars, believed that all heavenly motions were circular. But the Greeks had had a hard time explaining the strange motions of five special "stars." These stars were actually the planets Mercury, Venus, Mars, Jupiter, and Saturn. Before telescopes, these five objects looked to observers like all the other tiny lights in the sky, so people assumed the objects were stars.

These five planets moved a bit oddly. The other stars crossed the sky together from east to west, like lights attached to a moving dome. The odd planets traveled in loopy, wavy paths that drifted eastward against the dome of stars. So the ancient Greeks called these stars *planetes asteres*, or "wandering stars."

To explain the planets' motion, Eudoxus said that Earth lay still at the center of the universe. Several transparent spheres, one inside the other, enveloped Earth. Each sphere could spin in any direction. The outermost sphere carried the regular stars. Inside that, several more spheres carried the planets, the sun, and the moon.

Most Greek scholars agreed with Eudoxus. But one notable thinker who disagreed was Aristarchus. In the third century BCE, Aristarchus said that Earth was just one of many objects orbiting the sun. He suggested that the universe was heliocentric, or sun-centered, not geocentric. He said the motions of the moon, planets, stars, and the sun around Earth was an illusion. These objects only *seemed* to move through the sky because *Earth* was spinning. Aristarchus was right. But no one paid any attention to his ideas because they were so different from common beliefs at the time. If Earth was moving, people believed they should be able to feel the motion. And people should also notice a parallax, or difference in the apparent positions of nearby stars. The stars should appear to shift as Earth moved and people saw the stars from different locations.

Instead, scientists continued to promote and develop geocentric models of the universe. The most famous and influential of these thinkers was Ptolemy, who lived in Egypt in the second century CE. Then Egypt was part of the Roman Empire. Ptolemy expanded on Eudoxus's model using detailed, accurate measurements of star positions that had been made by Greek astronomer Hipparchus. Ptolemy believed that each planet traveled in a perfectly circular orbit around Earth. He explained the planets' loopy, wavy motions by saying that as each planet traveled its circular orbit, it also moved in a smaller circle. He called this smaller circle an epicycle.

The Christian Church approved of Ptolemy's theory because it explained the motions of the moon, planets, stars, and the sun without placing anything but an unmoving Earth at the center of

Greek thinker Claudius Ptolemy (90–168) proposed a geocentric theory of the universe. He believed Earth was at the center of the universe and all other planets orbited around Earth.

the universe. The idea of Earth lying still at the center of the universe was also found in the Christian Bible. Ptolemy's theory soon became an official Christian teaching. This cosmology dominated the Christian world for more than one thousand years.

NEW **IDEAS**

In the sixteenth century, scientists began questioning this geocentric cosmology. It began with the ideas of Nicolaus Copernicus. Although Copernicus worked as a church administrator in Poland, his true love was astronomy. He spent all his spare time studying the night sky and using mathematics to make sense of what he saw. He noticed that while Ptolemy's theory worked pretty well, it didn't explain all the details of planetary motion that Copernicus noticed. Copernicus's observations led him to develop the theory that Earth and the other planets orbited the sun and the moon orbited Earth—all in circular paths. His theory explained the odd paths of the planets across Earth's night sky in a simpler way than Ptolemy's theory did.

Copernicus first wrote about these ideas in 1514. But he didn't publish a book detailing his theory until 1543, just before his death. The book was titled *De Revolutionibus Orbium Coelestium* (On the Revolutions of the Heavenly Orbs). Copernicus died shortly after its publication.

Even though *De Revolutionibus* clearly contradicted the Bible as well as long-accepted scientific ideas, it didn't encounter much resistance at first. Many people simply accepted it as a formula to explain planetary motions. They didn't think Copernicus was saying that Earth *really* orbits the sun. Scholars sometimes

Nicolaus Copernicus created a circular diagram based on his studies of the night sky. Unlike Ptolemy, he believed that Earth and other planets orbited the sun and the moon orbited Earth.

MARTIN LUTHER'S VIEW

Martin Luther was the leader of the Protestant Reformation, a religious movement in Europe. Luther was vocal about his dislike of Copernicus and his ideas about Earth and its place in the universe: "There is talk of a new [astronomer] who wants to prove that the earth moves and goes round instead of the sky, sun and the moon, just as if somebody moving in a carriage or ship might hold that he was sitting still and at rest while the earth and trees walked and moved. But that is how things are nowadays: when a man wishes to be clever he must needs invent something special, and the way he does it must needs be the best! The fool wants to turn the whole art of astronomy upside-down."

made up scenarios in this way to explain complicated ideas and simplify calculations.

But several decades later, people began to realize what Copernicus meant and they began to rail against him. If the moon orbits Earth and Earth is moving, they said, why doesn't Earth leave the moon behind? If Earth is moving, why can a stone be thrown up and it falls straight down? Why does Copernicus's model predict the planets' positions only a little better than Ptolemy's? And how dare a man of the church defy the Bible?

Copernicus did not have many supporters in the late 1500s—at least not publicly. The first scientist to publicly endorse his ideas was Johannes Kepler, a German mathematician and Lutheran minister. Kepler began working for Danish astronomer Tycho Brahe in 1600. Tycho was famous for making the most accurate and complete astronomical measurements at the time. After Tycho died in 1601, his data went to Kepler. Using Copernicus's theory and Tycho's data, Kepler worked for eight years. He finally decided in 1609 that Copernicus had been right overall, but the planets' orbits were elliptical, not circular. That's why Copernicus's model didn't predict the planets' positions much better than Ptolemy's. This idea became the first of Kepler's three laws of planetary motion.

Italian scientist Galileo Galilei used Kepler's mathematical analysis in his own work. This analysis, as well as Kepler's support, turned out to be helpful to Galileo. Galileo was the first to study the skies with a telescope. Dutch eyeglass maker Hans Lippershey had just invented this tool in 1608, and in 1609, Galileo turned it toward the heavens. His observations provided new information that showed Ptolemy's geocentric model couldn't possibly be right.

Galileo found that the planets did not look at all like the stars. The stars looked like points of light, but the planets looked like illuminated globes. He concluded that the planets were not stars but, instead, were other worlds. He watched four lights that appeared to be moving around Jupiter. He proposed that the lights were moons orbiting the big planet. The latter observation, in particular, showed that Ptolemy hadn't known everything about the heavens. Clearly the skies contained objects Ptolemy had never seen. It also proved that a planet would not leave its moons behind as it orbited the sun. Furthermore, Galileo found that Venus underwent a set of phases, or changes in the way it looked from Earth. In an Earth-centered

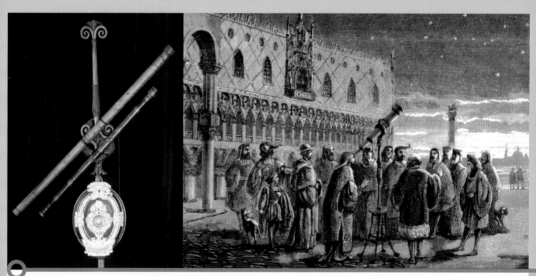

Galileo was the first to view the night sky through a telescope *(left)*. He used a different kind of telescope to point out Jupiter to a group of senators in Venice, Italy, in 1609 *(right)*.

system, viewers on Earth should always see Venus as a crescent, because the sun is beyond Venus. But in a sun-centered system, Venus viewed from Earth should change shapes as Earth's and Venus's positions changed in relation to the sun.

Galileo's belief in Copernican astronomy, which he published widely, got him into big trouble with the Roman Catholic Church. Despite more than twenty years of badgering, threats, and eventually condemnation and imprisonment in 1633, Galileo refused to back down. He agreed to sign a document saying he'd been wrong only after he'd grown old and ill. He knew this document didn't mean anything, because his ideas had already spread far and wide through his books and his supporters.

English scientist Isaac Newton later built on the ideas of Copernicus, Kepler, and Galileo. In 1687 Newton published his laws of motion. He showed that objects in the heavens and objects on Earth followed the same laws of motion. Gravity was the force responsible for the orbits of the planets around the sun and the orbit of the moon around Earth. Newton's laws of motion and gravitation explained the movements of the moon, planets, stars, and the sun better than any earlier theories.

By 1700 most educated people accepted the idea of a heliocentric solar system. The Roman Catholic Church reversed its ban on Copernican theory in 1758. More than two centuries later, in 1979, Pope John Paul II reopened the church's case against Galileo. In 1992 the church finally reversed Galileo's sentence. The church published an official apology to Galileo in 2000.

EVER-EXPANDING **VIEWS**

Since Galileo turned his telescope to the sky, the discoveries have never stopped. And as telescopes improved, scientists saw more objects and more details. They have continued to expand people's views of the solar system and the universe beyond.

After the 1781 discovery of Uranus, astronomers studying the planet with telescopes noticed an orbital wobble, or slight wiggle, in its orbital path. In theory, Uranus shouldn't wobble if only the sun's gravity and that of the six inner planets were pulling on it. So scientists guessed that a more distant planet must have a gravitational pull on Uranus. The 1846 discovery of Neptune explained some of the wobble, but not all of it. And Neptune's orbital path was a little wiggly too. Scientists figured that another planet lay beyond Neptune. In 1930 astronomer Clyde Tombaugh found it and named it Pluto.

During the 1970s, 1980s, 1990s, and early 2000s, powerful new telescopes revealed much more about the space beyond Neptune. They showed that Pluto and its three then-known moons were just four of about seventy thousand similar-sized icy objects in the area.

After these discoveries, in 2006 astronomers realized that they should define the criteria used to classify a planet. They decided that a planet must orbit the sun and have enough gravity to pull itself into a sphere. And a planet's gravity must have cleared its orbital region, meaning that it does not share its orbit with objects of a similar size and mass.

Pluto broke the last rule, as there are many objects in its orbit with similar size and mass. So Pluto is not a true planet. Instead, it is a dwarf planet. But it is still important to scientists. That's why the US space program sent a spacecraft to visit Pluto in 2006. The craft, *New Horizons*, is due to fly by Pluto in July 2015.

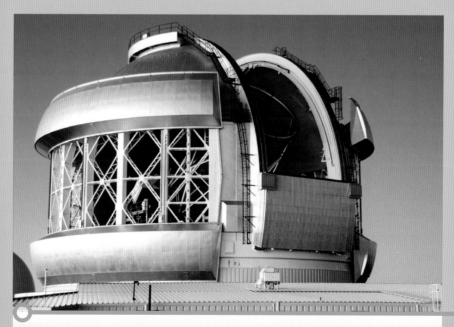

The Frederick C. Gillett Gemini North telescope sits atop Mauna Kea, a dormant volcano in Hawaii. Scientists used this huge telescope to capture detailed images of Pluto, which helped them decide that Pluto was not technically a planet.

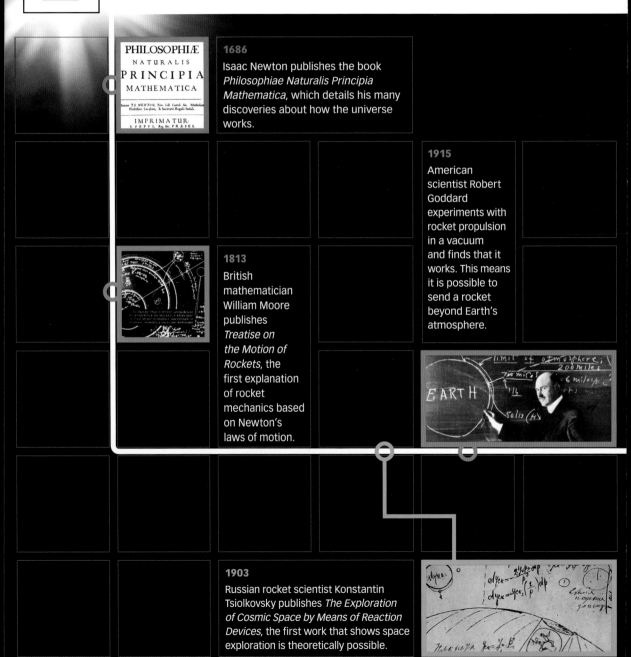

PHILOSOPHIÆ
NATURALIS
PRINCIPIA
MATHEMATICA·

Autore JS. NEWTON, Trin. Coll. Cantab. Soc. Mathesios Professore Lucasiano, & Societatis Regalis Sodali.

IMPRIMATUR·
S. PEPYS, Reg. Soc. PRÆSES.

1686
Isaac Newton publishes the book *Philosophiae Naturalis Principia Mathematica*, which details his many discoveries about how the universe works.

1915
American scientist Robert Goddard experiments with rocket propulsion in a vacuum and finds that it works. This means it is possible to send a rocket beyond Earth's atmosphere.

1813
British mathematician William Moore publishes *Treatise on the Motion of Rockets*, the first explanation of rocket mechanics based on Newton's laws of motion.

1903
Russian rocket scientist Konstantin Tsiolkovsky publishes *The Exploration of Cosmic Space by Means of Reaction Devices*, the first work that shows space exploration is theoretically possible.

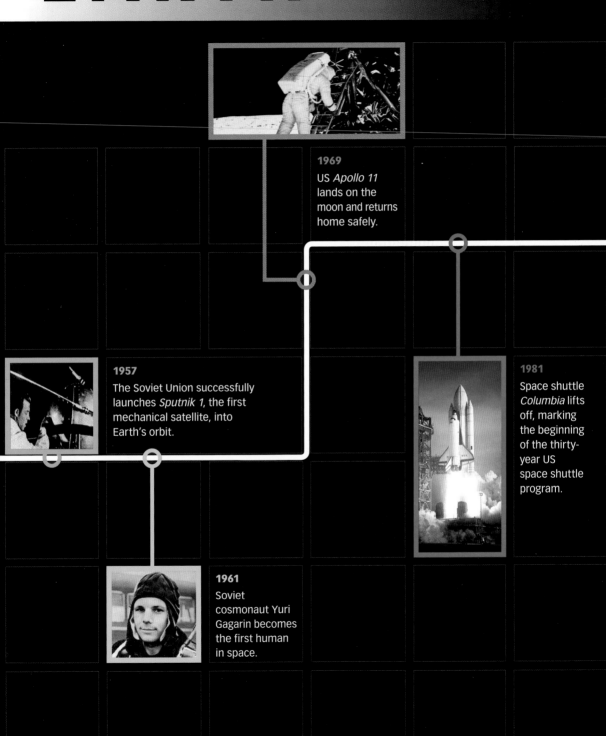

1969
US *Apollo 11* lands on the moon and returns home safely.

1957
The Soviet Union successfully launches *Sputnik 1*, the first mechanical satellite, into Earth's orbit.

1981
Space shuttle *Columbia* lifts off, marking the beginning of the thirty-year US space shuttle program.

1961
Soviet cosmonaut Yuri Gagarin becomes the first human in space.

While some scientists have poured their talents into studying the heavens, others have spent their lives trying to figure out how people might get there. And one scientist, Isaac Newton, built a bridge connecting the science of astronomy to the science of space travel. Newton's studies of the heavens and Earth uncovered the laws of motion that govern everything in the universe. Understanding these laws was the first step necessary for humans to leave Earth's orbit and explore the universe beyond.

NEWTON'S **LAWS**

In the 1670s and the 1680s, Newton was focused on understanding how the universe worked. He published his theories in 1686, in his book *Philosophiae Naturalis Principia Mathematica* (The Mathematical Principles of Natural Philosophy). Among many other things, this book stated three very important principles:

Isaac Newton developed three theories of motion, which he published in his 1686 book *Philosophiae Naturalis Principia Mathematica* (The Mathematical Principles of Natural Philosophy).

1. An object at rest stays at rest unless an unbalanced force acts on it. A moving object stays moving at the same speed and direction unless an unbalanced force acts on it.
2. When a force acts on an object, the force accelerates the object, or changes its speed and direction. The greater the object's mass, the more force is necessary to accelerate it.
3. Every action has an opposite and equal reaction.

A DRAWING POWER **IN MATTER**

William Stukeley was Isaac Newton's friend. According to legend, in 1726, while sitting under some apple trees in Newton's garden, Newton explained how a falling apple had once sparked his thinking about gravity. Here's part of what Stukeley wrote about that conversation: "'Why should that apple always descend perpendicularly to the ground,' thought [Newton] to himself: occasioned by the fall of an apple, as he sat in a contemplative mood. 'why should it not go sideways, or upwards? but constantly to the earths centre? assuredly, the reason is, that the earth draws it. there must be a drawing power in matter. & the sum of the drawing power in the matter of the earth must be in the earths centre, not in any side of the earth.'"

While forming these principles, Newton also came up with his famous ideas about gravity. Legend has it that an apple inspired him. Newton supposedly saw an apple fall from a tree. Since the apple's speed changed from zero (as it hung on the tree) to moving (as it fell), it accelerated. So, according to Newton's first law, a force must have acted on the apple to make it accelerate. He called that force gravity.

Newton's universal law of gravitation states that every object pulls on every other object. The amount of pull an object has depends on its mass. The more mass an object has, the more it pulls on other objects. And the closer two objects are, the more strongly they pull on each other. The force weakens quickly as the distance between objects grows.

What does this have to do with space travel? Newton's cannonball example makes that clear. Imagine, he said, an extremely tall mountain with a cannon on its summit. Someone fires a cannonball horizontally from it. Earth's gravity pulls on the cannonball. Its path curves downward until it meets the ground. Imagine someone putting more gunpowder in the cannon and shooting another cannonball. This time, it goes farther but still hits the ground. Finally, imagine using a huge amount of gunpowder. This time, the cannonball travels so far that its curved path parallels Earth's curved surface. The cannonball keeps falling, but Earth's surface keeps curving away, so the cannonball never hits the ground. It just

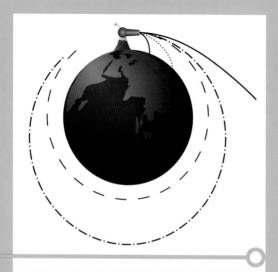
Newton used the example of a cannonball launched from a tall mountain to explain how objects orbit one another.

keeps falling and falling, circling Earth endlessly. Space stations and satellites orbit Earth in the same way. This is also how the moon orbits Earth and how planets, comets, and asteroids orbit the sun.

Thanks to Newton, humans understand the laws of motion that all objects—from people to planets—follow. To orbit Earth, one must get *just* far enough away from Earth's surface. And to leave Earth completely, one must escape Earth's orbit. This knowledge made space travel possible. But it took nearly three centuries for space travel to actually happen.

THE SCIENCE **OF ROCKETRY**

First, scientists had to figure out whether it was possible to launch an object from Earth with enough force to put it into orbit—or beyond. People had been making rockets ever since the eleventh century, when Chinese engineers mixed charcoal, saltpeter, and sulfur to make gunpowder, a fuel for rockets used in warfare. It wasn't until the nineteenth century, however, that scientists closely studied how and why rockets work.

In 1813 British mathematician William Moore published *Treatise on the Motion of Rockets*, the first explanation of rocket mechanics based on Newton's laws of motion. Ninety years later, in 1903, Russian rocket scientist Konstantin Tsiolkovsky expanded on that knowledge by publishing *The Exploration of Cosmic Space by Means of Reaction Devices*. This was the first work that showed space exploration was theoretically possible. Tsiolkovsky's article explained how to achieve liftoff with liquid fuels. He suggested using multistage rockets, which would be discarded as they used up their fuel. He developed methods and formulas for adjusting a spacecraft's speed and direction that modern scientists still use.

Scientists had figured out that space travel was possible. Next, American physicist Robert Goddard pushed space travel closer to reality by advancing the science of rocketry. Among many other contributions, in 1915 Goddard experimented with rocket propulsion in a vacuum. He found that it worked, which meant it was possible to send a rocket beyond Earth's atmosphere, because space is also a vacuum. In 1919 he published *A Method of Reaching Extreme Altitudes.* This book laid out Goddard's mathematical theories explaining how rockets flew. It also described his research on rockets propelled by solid fuel and liquid fuel. Seven years later, in 1926, he launched the first liquid-fuel rocket.

In the 1930s, Hermann Oberth and his colleague Wernher von Braun studied Goddard's work and built upon it to develop the V-2 rocket. On October 3, 1942, Germany launched the V-2. It was the first human-made object to achieve spaceflight. It reached an altitude of 62 miles (100 kilometers), considered the rough boundary between Earth's atmosphere

Robert Goddard, a physics professor at Clark University in Massachussetts, developed mathematical theories to explain how rockets flew.

The V-2 rocket, developed by German scientists Wernher von Braun and Hermann Oberth, was the first human-made object to reach the boundary between Earth's atmosphere and outer space, in 1942.

and outer space. The V-2 became the model for all rockets that followed. In 1945 von Braun left Germany with dozens of other German specialists to work for the US Army. In 1955 Oberth joined them. This team developed the Saturn family of rockets, which became a key element of the US space program.

THE RACE **TO SPACE**

Meanwhile, the United States' archrival at the time, the Soviet Union (a union of fifteen republics that included Russia), was developing its own space program. On October 4, 1957, the Soviet Union successfully launched the first human-made satellite into Earth's orbit—*Sputnik 1*. It was an aluminum ball about 23 inches (58 centimeters) in diameter, with four long antennae. It weighed 184 pounds (83 kilograms). It orbited Earth for about three months, transmitting data about the upper atmosphere for the first twenty-two days. Just a month later, on November 3, the Soviet Union launched *Sputnik 2*. This craft was much larger—about 6 feet (2 meters) wide and 13 feet (4 m) tall. It carried the dog Laika, the first animal in space. Although Laika lived only a few hours in space due to a cooling failure and stress, she proved that a living creature could tolerate space travel.

The Sputnik launches caught the whole world off guard. US officials were especially alarmed. The Soviet Union had not only beaten the United States into space with much larger craft than the United States had developed, but the Soviet Union had also developed very powerful rockets. The US government worried that this meant the Soviet Union

Soviet pilot Yuri Gagarin *(left)* was the first human to venture into space in 1961. Eight years later, Buzz Aldrin *(right)* walked on the moon with Neil Armstrong. Aldrin and Armstrong were crew members of the *Apollo 11*, the first manned spacecraft to land on the moon.

could launch bombs that would travel all the way to the United States. In response, the United States immediately established the National Aeronautics and Space Administration (NASA) and kicked its space program into high gear. The US-Soviet Space Race, a competition for spaceflight achievements, began.

Throughout the late 1950s and the 1960s, American and Soviet scientists logged dozens of firsts. In 1959 the Soviets launched *Luna 1*, the first human-made object to exit Earth's orbit. In September *Luna 2* intentionally crash-landed on the moon, becoming the first spacecraft to make contact there. That year the United States launched its first spy satellite and took the first photos of Earth from space. In 1960 the United States launched the first weather satellite. In 1961 Soviet cosmonaut Yuri Gagarin became the first human in space, followed a few weeks later by American astronaut Alan Shepard. That year, US president John F. Kennedy promised that by the end of the 1960s, an American would land on the moon and return home safely. In 1962 the United States launched the first communications satellite. Three years later, in 1965, Soviet cosmonaut Alexei Leonov made the first spacewalk. In 1966 the Soviet

Union's unmanned *Venera 3* probe landed on Venus, becoming the first craft to make contact with another planet. And in 1969, the US *Apollo 11* crew landed on the moon and returned home safely, fulfilling Kennedy's promise.

SPACE
EXPLORATION

Throughout the 1970s, the US Apollo missions and the Soviet Luna missions continued to explore the moon. The Soviet Union also continued its Venera missions to Venus, managing to land craft that survived the intense heat and pressure long enough to transmit data back to Earth from Venus's surface. Meanwhile, some scientists turned their attention to new projects.

Scientists knew people could survive a relatively brief space voyage, as a trip to the moon took three days. But what about visiting space for a longer time? The Soviets were the first to answer this question. They launched the first Earth-orbiting space station, the *Salyut 1*, in 1971. Soviet cosmonauts lived and worked aboard it for three weeks. The engineering tests they performed and the failures they experienced, such as problems with docking, helped them develop

Salyut 1 (top), the first Earth-orbiting space station, demonstrated that people could survive in space for three weeks. The first space shuttle *(bottom)* was designed to carry cargo into space and then return it to Earth.

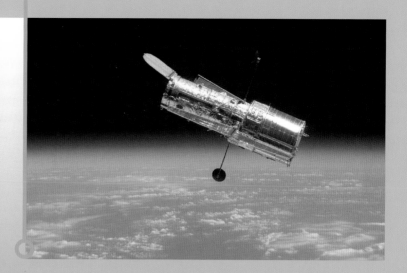

The Hubble Space Telescope (hovering 353 miles, or 568 km, above Earth's surface) takes clear, sharp images of outer space, which are useful to astronomers.

better space stations afterward. Later stations built by the Soviet Union and other countries permitted longer stays and safer and more efficient docking, supply, and passenger transport systems.

In 1972 President Richard Nixon announced that NASA would begin developing a new kind of launch vehicle, a reusable space shuttle. It launched vertically, like a rocket, and returned to Earth horizontally, like an airplane. It was designed to carry not only astronauts but also large cargoes, such as satellites, into orbit and bring them back to Earth. In 1981 space shuttle *Columbia* lifted off. This marked the beginning of a thirty-year program. From 1981 to 2011, NASA's fleet of five shuttles flew 135 missions. These missions deployed many satellites, built the International Space Station (ISS), carried staff and supplies to the ISS, and launched the Hubble Space Telescope in 1990.

The Hubble, a collaboration of NASA and the European Space Agency (ESA), is extremely valuable to astronomers. It can take supersharp images of outer space with almost no interference from background light, which occurs in images taken from Earth's surface using telescopes. It allows humans a deep view into space. Space telescopes such as the Hubble and its successor, the James Webb Space Telescope slated for launch in 2018, show how astronomy and space travel are intertwined. Thanks to astronomy, space travel became possible. And thanks to space travel, a vast amount of information about the distant reaches of our universe is available to modern astronomers.

1596

Dutch mapmaker Abraham Ortelius notices that the eastern coastlines of the Americas match up with the western coastlines of Europe and Africa.

1912

German scientist Alfred Wegener suggests that Earth's continents were once joined and gradually moved apart over millions of years.

1800s

Most geologists believe that gradual processes shape Earth over vast spans of time and that the continents have been in the same places since Earth's formation.

CONTOURS

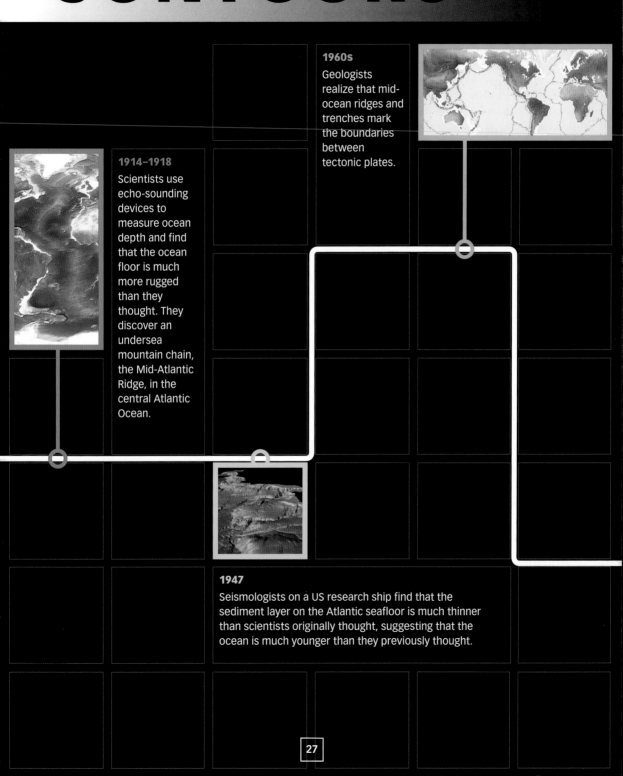

1960s
Geologists realize that mid-ocean ridges and trenches mark the boundaries between tectonic plates.

1914–1918
Scientists use echo-sounding devices to measure ocean depth and find that the ocean floor is much more rugged than they thought. They discover an undersea mountain chain, the Mid-Atlantic Ridge, in the central Atlantic Ocean.

1947
Seismologists on a US research ship find that the sediment layer on the Atlantic seafloor is much thinner than scientists originally thought, suggesting that the ocean is much younger than they previously thought.

Thousands of years ago, humans had a very different concept of the world than modern humans have. They assumed that the world consisted of whatever they could see for themselves, learn about from their neighbors, or use logic to imagine.

THE SHAPE OF **EARTH**

During the first millennium BCE, the ancient Greeks knew about most of Europe and some of Asia and Africa. Since they believed that Earth was a sphere and that Earth's land must be in balance around the globe, they reasoned that all the land in the Northern Hemisphere must be balanced by a similar amount of land in Earth's Southern Hemisphere. Greek mapmaker Ptolemy illustrated this belief on his maps in the second century CE. In his maps, the Indian Ocean was completely surrounded by Africa, India, and a southern land that stretched all the way to the South Pole.

For centuries, most Europeans imagined Earth this way. People who lived in other parts of the world saw Earth differently. But no one had a complete or correct image. That's because back then, a person's

Ptolemy's map illustrates what the ancient Greeks imagined the world looked like, with equal landmass in the Northern and Southern Hemispheres.

Abraham Ortelius believed that earthquakes and floods had separated the Americas from Europe and Africa. His sixteenth-century map depicts the way the continents' shapes could fit together like a jigsaw puzzle.

worldview was limited. Travel and communication were both difficult. People couldn't see much of the world and couldn't easily share ideas with others elsewhere.

During the Middle Ages (about 500 to 1500), Arab, Chinese, and European traders began exploring Earth intensely by sea and land. With each voyage, human knowledge of Earth grew. By the mid-1800s, most people agreed on the general shapes and locations of Earth's lands and oceans.

THEORIES OF **CONTINENT FORMATION**

Long before scholars figured out the contours of Earth, scientists began to notice something really interesting: the continents' shapes fit together like a jigsaw puzzle. Dutch mapmaker Abraham Ortelius first wrote about this. In 1596 he suggested that the Americas were "torn away from Europe and Africa . . . by earthquakes and floods" and that "the [traces] of the rupture reveal themselves, if someone brings forward a map of the world and considers carefully the coasts of the three [continents]."

Ortelius's idea dovetailed nicely with a scientific theory that developed about two centuries later. This theory, called catastrophism, said that a series of huge, short, global upheavals had changed Earth dramatically and created mountains, valleys, and other large landforms. Geologists study the history of Earth and its life through evidence contained in rocks. Geologists saw that different layers of rock contained unique sets of fossils. These scientists concluded that the fossils of each layer were animals that once lived and then went extinct because of some catastrophe. This theory's biggest promoter was French naturalist Georges Cuvier, who lived in the late 1700s and the early 1800s.

But by the mid-1800s, most scientists had rejected the theory of catastrophism. Instead, they supported a theory called uniformitarianism. The term *uniformitarianism* came from the concept of uniform processes. In the 1790s, a Scottish geologist named James Hutton proposed that gradual processes, such as slow erosion of a coast by waves, shaped Earth over a vast period of time. Hutton believed the processes in the past were the same processes of the present—rivers, tides, volcanoes, waves, and so on. In the early 1800s, British geologist Charles Lyell set out to find evidence for uniformitarianism. He found clues that sea levels had risen and fallen many times, large volcanoes had formed on top of much older rocks, and other gradual changes had occurred over long periods of time. This evidence, published in the three-volume work *Principles of Geology* (1830–1833), persuaded most of his peers and later geologists.

Uniformitarianists believed that the continents had always been in the same places. So in the early twentieth century, most geologists thought that continents could rise and fall, but not move horizontally.

ALL OF THE **ABOVE**

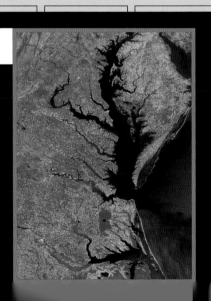

Modern scientists say that the catastrophists and the uniformitarianists were both right— and both wrong. Gradual geologic processes did shape Earth over long periods of time. But catastrophic events, such as collisions with large meteors, do occur, and these events are important too. These rare catastrophes have affected our planet dramatically. For example, a meteor impact near modern Norfolk, Virginia, 35 million years ago left a huge crater. About ten thousand years ago, ice sheets melted, filling in the crater and forming Chesapeake Bay *(right).*

They said Earth was slowly cooling down and shrinking. This shrinkage caused wrinkles in the surface. People knew these wrinkles as mountains. Geologists explained matching features on different continents, such as the many matching fossils and rock formations on the east coast of South America and the west coast of Africa, by saying that land bridges had once connected the continents. These bridges could no longer be seen because they had worn away over time.

FROM CONTINENTAL DRIFT
TO PLATE TECTONICS

German scientist Alfred Wegener was not convinced by these ideas. He did not think that huge land bridges were very likely. And if they had worn away as suggested, why did the coastlines of the Americas match those of Europe and Africa so closely? Erosion probably would not have created the same coastal curves so far apart over such a long time. Wegener also didn't think that the cooling and shrinking theory explained why mountains existed only in certain areas or why some mountains were very old while others were relatively young. If Earth were shrinking and wrinkling, mountains should be spread evenly around the globe and they should all be roughly the same age.

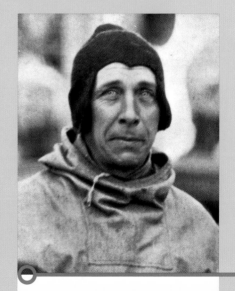

German scientist Alfred Wegener developed the theory of continental drift. He hypothesized that Earth's continents were once joined in one landmass, but that they'd moved apart over time.

In 1912 Wegener came up with a new explanation for the shapes, locations, and features of the continents. He said that Earth's continents were once joined. They gradually moved apart over millions of years. Wegener thought mountains formed when the edge of one continent crashed into another, causing crumpling. For example, the Himalayas formed when India crashed into Asia. Wegener called his theory "continental drift." He couldn't explain what force was strong enough to move continents, though. So most of the scientific community just laughed at him at first. But in the end, Wegener was proven right. New geologists steadily gathered proof that plate tectonics, or movement of huge plates of Earth's crust, had happened and was still happening.

First, engineers invented technology for mapping the ocean floor. During World War I (1914–1918), scientists used echo-sounding devices to measure ocean depth. They recorded the time it took for a sound signal to leave the ship, bounce off the seafloor, and return to the ship. Charts of the timing of the returned signals showed that the seafloor was much rougher than people had thought. The measurements clearly showed an undersea mountain chain in the central Atlantic Ocean—the Mid-Atlantic Ridge. Before this, no one really knew what was down there. People generally pictured the seafloor as flat, smooth, and boring, like a giant bathtub.

This topographic image of the Atlantic Ocean seafloor shows the ocean's depth. The ocean is deepest in the dark blue areas. The light blue line that snakes through the central Atlantic Ocean is the Mid-Atlantic Ridge.

Then, in 1947, seismologists on a US research ship discovered that the sediment on the Atlantic seafloor was much thinner than scientists had once thought. This meant that the ocean had not existed in its modern form for nearly as long as they had thought. Scientists believed that the oceans were at least 4 billion years old and that the sediment should have been quite thick.

Throughout the 1960s, geologists gathered evidence that showed the youngest regions of the ocean floor were the mid-ocean ridges. This evidence also showed that the oldest regions were in deep-sea trenches—deep, narrow undersea canyons. Scientists proposed that mid-ocean ridges were weak areas in the ocean floor, where it broke in two along ridge crests. They said new magma from deep inside Earth rose through the weak spots and erupted along the crests to create new parts of Earth's crust. The new oceanic crust spreads away from the ridges like a conveyor belt. Millions of years later, the oceanic crust descends into the trenches.

In 1963 the World-Wide Standardized Seismograph Network (WWSSN) was established. Data from WWSSN instruments allowed scientists to make precise maps of earthquake activity around the world. Scientists found evidence of earthquakes happening continually along the oceanic ridges and trenches. These ridges and trenches, they said, mark the boundaries between tectonic plates.

HOW **PLATE TECTONICS** WORK

Earthquakes, mountains, and volcanoes are all found at the boundaries between tectonic plates. Which phenomenon happens depends on the direction the plates are moving. If the plates are moving apart, the movement creates volcanoes. This happens at the Mid-Atlantic Ridge and in East Africa. If the plates are moving together, the edges of the plates crumple. One plate burrows under the other. This produces trenches and mountains. The friction can also melt rocks and create volcanoes. It happens along the west coast of the Americas, the east coasts of Asia and Australia, and in the Himalayas. If the plates are moving sideways, tension builds at the boundary between the plates. At some point, the plates suddenly slip. This slippage is an earthquake. Earthquakes happen along the San Andreas Fault in California, among other places.

For decades, scientists thought that Earth was the only planet in the solar system with plate tectonics. But in 2012, An Yin, a geologist at the University of California–Los Angeles, discovered that plate tectonics exist on Mars as well. Yin studied satellite images of Mars and saw features that looked a lot like Earth's fault systems. He saw a very long, deep, smooth, flat-sided canyon wall, which could only be formed by a fault. He also saw linear volcanic zones, a telltale sign of tectonic plates spreading apart. Yin thinks the crust of Mars consists of only two tectonic plates, compared to Earth's seven. And while Earth's plates are constantly active, Mars's plates are less active. They shift and cause Mars quakes only every million years or so.

1820s–1830s

Swiss paleontologist Louis Agassiz concludes that a great ice age once gripped Earth. French physicist Jean-Baptiste Joseph Fourier says atmospheric gases trap and hold a certain amount of heat near Earth's surface.

1859

Irish scientist John Tyndall finds that water vapor and carbon dioxide (CO_2) can absorb and trap heat and suggests that changes in these gases could change Earth's climate.

1890s

Swedish scientist Arvid Högbom estimates that humans add about as much CO_2 as all natural processes combined. Svante Arrhenius concludes that adding CO_2 to the atmosphere raises Earth's average temperature.

1938

British engineer and amateur meteorologist Guy Stewart Callendar concludes that burning fossil fuels has added enough CO_2 to Earth's air to raise Earth's average surface temperature.

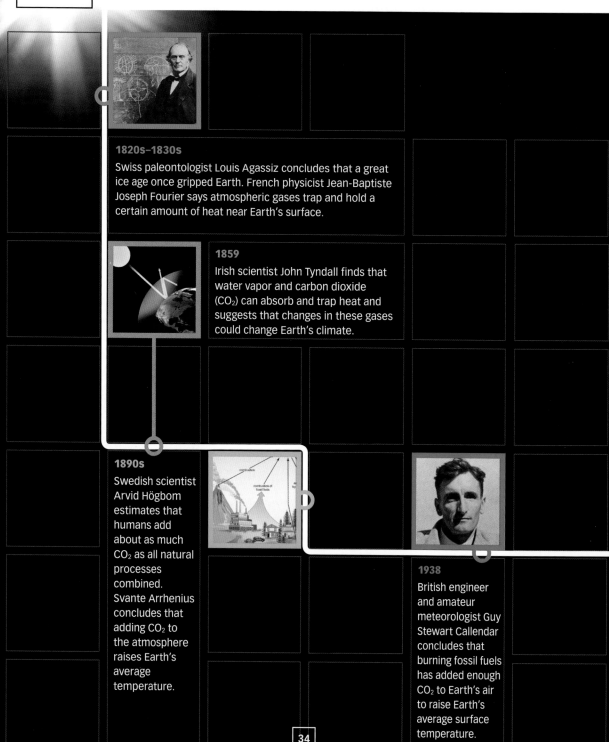

1990
The Intergovernmental Panel on Climate Change issues its first report. Four more follow, each more certain about the evidence.

1958
American geochemist Charles David Keeling starts collecting global air samples and measuring CO_2.

1980s
As accurate climate models become available, more scientists agree with and speak up about the reality of global warming and the potential for problems due to climate change.

1957
American chemists Hans Suess and Roger Revelle test seawater samples and find that oceans are not absorbing excess CO_2. They conclude that atmospheric CO_2 will keep increasing and Earth will keep warming.

Until a few centuries ago, most people thought that Earth's climate had always been more or less the same. But when scientists began studying Earth's glaciers in the early 1800s, that idea began to change.

CHANGEABLE **CLIMATE**

It started with the work of Swiss paleontologist Louis Agassiz. While Agassiz examined the geological features of his home country, he noticed signs of glaciers where no glaciers currently existed. These signs included huge valleys, large boulders that didn't match their surroundings, scratched and smoothed rock surfaces, and mounds of debris. He went on to find these signs throughout Europe and North America. In the 1830s, he concluded that Earth had once endured a great ice age.

That glaciers had once advanced and retreated across Earth suggested that Earth's climate *could* change. It had once been cold enough to form continent-size glaciers. Then it warmed up enough to melt most of the glaciers. Not only did the climate change, but it had done so many times.

The Vatnajökull glacier *(left)* is the largest glacier in Iceland and is evidence of the great ice age that Louis Agassiz *(right)* believed had rearranged Earth's landscape.

HOW THE **GREENHOUSE EFFECT WORKS**

The sun continually gives off huge amounts of energy. Solar energy includes both visible light and invisible energy, such as heat and ultraviolet radiation. Earth's atmosphere lets solar energy pass through. Clouds, ice, and snow are white, a color that reflects some of the energy back to space. Darker things, such as buildings, land, trees, or water, absorb a lot of energy.

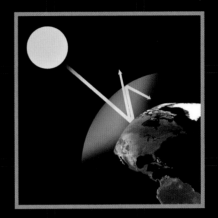

As Earth absorbs energy, Earth's surface warms up. As Earth's surface cools down, it gives off heat. Some heat escapes Earth's atmosphere. Some heat gets absorbed by gases in the atmosphere, which then give off that heat again. They do this over and over, trapping heat in the atmosphere. This process is what makes Earth warm enough for living things to survive.

Scientists then had no idea how this had happened. Primitive humans certainly couldn't have caused it, they thought. The scientists proposed other causes: variations in the sun's heat, erupting volcanoes, mountain ranges growing and shrinking and changing ocean currents and wind patterns, and changes in the makeup of the air. But nobody knew for sure.

While some scientists were puzzling over glaciers, others were studying gases. In the 1820s, French physicist Jean-Baptiste Joseph Fourier wondered why Earth stayed so warm. His calculations told him that, given Earth's large size, its distance from the sun, and the fact that Earth is warmed only by sunlight, the planet should be a lot colder. Fourier analyzed an experiment another scientist had done to measure the intensity of sunlight on Earth's surface. The scientist had used a device enclosed in glass to see how high the temperature rose. Fourier proposed that like the glass in this device, gases in Earth's atmosphere trapped some heat near Earth's surface. This heat-trapping effect later became known as the greenhouse effect. The gases that trap heat were called greenhouse gases.

In 1859 Irish scientist John Tyndall performed experiments to measure the ability of different gases to absorb and radiate heat. He found that oxygen, nitrogen, and hydrogen have a little of this ability, but water vapor and carbon dioxide (CO_2) have a lot. He said that without the latter, Earth would be "held fast in the iron grip of frost." He also noted that changes in water vapor and CO_2 could have caused "all the mutations of climate which the researches of geologists reveal."

By the late 1800s, scientists knew that not only could Earth's climate change but also that changes in the makeup of the atmosphere could cause climate change. But how could the atmosphere change?

In the 1890s, the work of two scientists pointed the way to an answer. The first was Swedish scientist Arvid Högbom. He estimated how much CO_2 passes into and out of the atmosphere from all processes in the carbon cycle. He recognized that coal-burning factories, which at the time were burning hundreds of millions of tons of coal per year, were pouring CO_2 into the air. He estimated that industry was adding about as much CO_2 as all natural processes together. Högbom's colleague, Svante Arrhenius, studied Högbom's calculations. Arrhenius concluded that as humans burned fossil fuels, they would add CO_2 to Earth's atmosphere and raise the planet's average temperature.

Arrhenius wasn't the least bit worried about this possibility. He had been searching for evidence to explain the ice ages. He was far more concerned about that type of climate change. He thought that in thousands of years—but certainly not anytime soon—burning fossil fuels might help prevent a future ice age. It might even improve the climate and crop yields. He didn't consider global warming a threat, and neither did most of his peers.

EVIDENCE OF **GLOBAL WARMING**

In the 1930s, an interesting new piece of evidence emerged. Guy Stewart Callendar, a British steam power engineer who studied weather and climate as a hobby, was the one who found it. He gathered temperature and CO_2 records going back to the year 1900. When he studied these records, he noticed that both temperature and CO_2 had been rising steadily. In 1938 Callendar concluded that the burning of fossil fuels had added

CARBON, CARBON DIOXIDE, AND THE CARBON CYCLE

All living or once-living things contain carbon. Soil contains carbon because dead organisms usually end up in the soil. Fossil fuels such as coal, oil, and natural gas contain huge amounts of carbon because they are the remains of plants and animals that died millions of years ago. Earth's oceans contain vast amounts of carbon too—both in the water and in the seafloor sediment.

Carbon dioxide is an odorless, colorless gas. It's made up of carbon (C) and oxygen (O). CO_2 is an important part of life on Earth. It is constantly cycling through the natural world. When the cells of living things turn food into energy, they release CO_2 as waste. When organisms die, they produce CO_2 as they rot. Tilling soil releases CO_2. So does burning pretty much anything. Plants, algae, and some microbes take in CO_2. They use it in a process called photosynthesis. They use energy from sunlight to change water and carbon dioxide into oxygen and sugar.

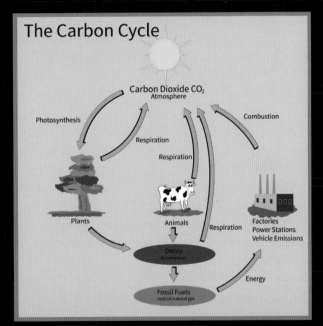

The Carbon Cycle

Carbon Dioxide CO_2
Atmosphere

Photosynthesis

Respiration

Respiration

Combustion

Plants

Animals

Respiration

Decay
decomposers

Fossil Fuels
coal/oil/natural gas

Energy

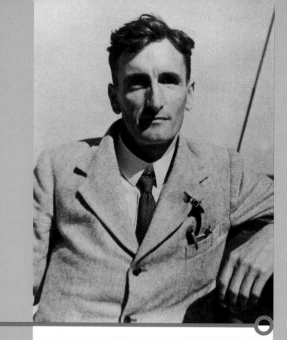

Guy Stewart Callendar researched CO_2 records and found that the burning of fossil fuels had increased atmospheric CO_2 and raised Earth's average surface temperature.

enough CO_2 to Earth's air that it had indeed raised Earth's average surface temperature. Scientific attitudes toward the possibility of global warming stayed the same, though. Everyone—including Callendar—thought that if global warming kept up for the next few centuries, that was probably a good thing.

Up until the 1950s, one reason people weren't concerned about global warming was that they believed oceans would absorb excess CO_2 from the atmosphere. American chemists Hans Suess and Roger Revelle disproved this idea. They tested many samples of ocean water and found that oceans were releasing nearly as much CO_2 as they absorbed. Meanwhile, humans were pouring more and more CO_2 into the air. Revelle and Suess concluded that atmospheric CO_2 would keep increasing and Earth would keep warming.

To prove whether CO_2 really was accumulating, scientists needed more accurate measurements than Callendar had been able to gather. Revelle convinced American geochemist Charles David Keeling to take on this task. In 1958 Keeling started collecting air samples from remote locations far from sources of air pollution. Keeling spent the rest of his career working on this, and others carried on with it after his 2005 death. By the 1970s, this data had proved that atmospheric CO_2 was increasing year by year.

Meanwhile, other scientists were designing mathematical models of the climate. These models used past weather and climate data to predict future weather and climate. Scientists discovered that climate is a very delicate and complex system. The models predicted that Earth's average surface temperature would warm enough to cause serious problems for living things. But because climate is so complex and the models were fairly new, many people had a hard time believing that the models were right.

It didn't help that temperature records from the 1940s to the early 1970s showed Earth's average surface temperature had dropped slightly during this period. Scientists quickly figured out that air pollution had caused this cooling. For a few decades, until more stringent laws reduced pollution, it had shaded Earth by blocking sunlight from reaching Earth's surface. This shading worked against global warming. Global warming started up again in the 1970s. But media reports on this issue had encouraged public doubt over whether it was really happening.

By the 1980s, scientists were able to gather more and better climate data from the distant past. They studied the chemistry of tree rings, ancient pollen, fossil shells, and ancient ice drilled from deep inside the Antarctic ice sheet. The data they collected helped them create better climate models. Meanwhile, temperatures kept rising, and the effects of warming on the environment were starting to show. Glaciers were melting faster, sea levels were rising, summers were warmer, and ecosystems were changing. Scientists grew more concerned about global warming and its effects. Some started speaking out. In 1988 the public started paying attention. That was largely because that summer was the hottest on record up to that time. An international group of scientists warned that the world should work to cut emissions of greenhouse gases into the atmosphere.

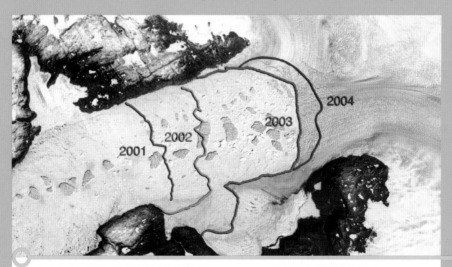

This is a satellite image of Jakobshavn Isbrae in Greenland, the fastest-moving glacier in the world. The lines illustrate where the ice has been calving, or breaking off into the ocean, from 2001 to 2004.

Many businesses and people simply didn't want to do so because it would cost a lot of money and would require lifestyle changes—or they opposed government regulation in general. So they complained loudly, spending millions of dollars to convince people that global warming was not a problem. A lot of people listened. And many questions remained in the scientific details. Different scientific assumptions about the impact of clouds and pollution produced slightly different predictions. A few degrees' difference meant very different effects on the environment. It was hard to know exactly what governments should do to help.

So the governments of the world formed a panel to give advice that would be as reliable as possible. Thousands of climate experts and officials worked out this advice together, using the most reliable and up-to-date technology and data. This panel is called the Intergovernmental Panel on Climate Change (IPCC). Since 1990 the IPCC has issued five reports, each carrying a message stronger than the last. The latest report, issued in 2014, said that global warming has clearly affected Earth's natural systems and human societies. It also said that if people do not try harder to adapt to these changes and prevent the worst effects, global warming could be disastrous.

GLOBAL WARMING'S **EFFECTS**

According to the IPCC's latest report, the effects of global warming and the climate change it brings will vary over time and in different places. These effects will depend on the steps people take to deal with them now. Here are some of the negative effects the IPCC predicts:

- North America: Shrinking snowpack in the mountains; and more frequent, intense, and prolonged heat waves in heat-prone areas
- Central and South America: Tropical rain forests gradually replaced by drier savannas; species extinctions in many tropical areas; and big changes in the amount of water available for drinking, farm irrigation, and generating electricity through waterpower
- Europe: Higher risk of flash floods inland, coastal flooding more often, more erosion from storms and rising seas, glaciers disappearing, less snow and tourism in the winter, species extinctions, and lower crop yields in southern Europe

A Kenyan woman washes clothes after a downpour in March 2014 ended a twelve-month drought.

- Africa: Severe water shortages, crop yields cut in half, and severe food shortages
- Asia: Shrinking freshwater supplies, more flooding in coastal areas, and a higher death rate resulting from disease linked with floods and droughts

LIMITLESS **POSSIBILITIES**

The development of astronomy, space travel, plate tectonics, and climatology make up just four of countless chapters in the story of Earth and space science. But these chapters illustrate some important common threads that run through all Earth and space science studies.

Although scientists have learned a lot about the universe over the past few centuries, the story of Earth and space science isn't over. This story is as old as humankind, and it will go on as long as humans do.

New discoveries in geology, climatology, oceanography, astronomy, and more make the potential for future discoveries seem limitless. But remember that no Earth or space science discoveries ever happen independently. Every new discovery or theory is part of a much larger structure of ideas. Every new idea is built upon a foundation that reaches deep into history. Key events in Earth and space science happen because of the events that happened before them.

YOUR TURN ON THE TIMELINE

Milestones in Earth and space science are not just a list of dates. They are events that affect people's day-to-day lives. Use what you have learned in this book to compose a diary entry.

First, pick one of the events listed on the timelines at the beginning of each chapter. Next, imagine what it was like to live during that time. Choose a person who was involved in the discovery or accomplishment. Or make up a character that this breakthrough affected. For example, pretend you are Galileo's daughter, or imagine you are an astronaut on one of the Apollo missions. Then write a diary entry or a series of entries about the event you have chosen. Your essay should show how this discovery affects the person's life. Include plenty of concrete details, so your readers will feel as if they were there.

After you finish writing, visit your local library or jump online. Try to find stories related to the historical event you selected. How do those stories compare with yours?

SOURCE NOTES

12 Martin Luther, *The Table-Talk of Martin Luther*, 1566, accessed June 22, 2014, http://www.lutherdansk.dk/Table-Talk/index1.htm.

19 Glenn Elert, "Universal Gravitation," *The Physics Hypertextbook*, accessed June 24, 2014, http://physics.info/gravitation/.

29 W. Jacquelyne Kious and Robert I. Tilling, "This Dynamic Earth: The Story of Plate Tectonics; Historical Perspective," US Geological Survey, August 7, 2012, http://pubs.usgs.gov/gip/dynamic/historical.html.

38 Charles Ichoku, "John Tyndall (1820–1893)," NASA Earth Observatory, accessed June 28, 2014, http://earthobservatory.nasa.gov/Features/Tyndall/.

38 Hervé Le Treut, Richard Somerville, Ulrich Cubasch, Yihui Ding, Cecilie Mauritzen, Abdalah Mokssit, Thomas Peterson, and Michael Prather, "Historical Overview of Climate Change Science," Intergovernmental Panel on Climate Change, 2007, accessed June 28, 2014, https://www.ipcc.ch/pdf/assessment -report/ar4/wg1/ar4-wg1-chapter1.pdf.

GLOSSARY

celestial: having to do with the sky or heavens

elliptical: in an oval shape

erosion: gradual wearing away of rock or soil by water, wind, or ice

fault: a break in Earth's surface that can cause earthquakes

orbit: an invisible path that an object travels around a planet or star

paleontologist: a scientist who studies the life of the distant past, especially from fossil remains

phase: a stage in the moon's or a planet's shape as seen from Earth

propulsion: the action of pushing or driving something forward in a certain direction

satellite: a heavenly body orbiting another of larger size, or a human-made object or vehicle intended to orbit Earth, the moon, or another heavenly body

seismologist: a scientist who studies earthquakes

species: a category of living things that have shared characteristics and that can mate and have offspring

technology: a machine, piece of equipment, or method designed by humans to do useful things

SELECTED BIBLIOGRAPHY

"Geology: Plate Tectonics." University of California Museum of Paleontology. Accessed September 14, 2014. http://www.ucmp.berkeley.edu/geology/tectonics.html.

Kious, W. Jacquelyne, and Robert I. Tilling. "This Dynamic Earth: The Story of Plate Tectonics; Historical Perspective." US Geological Survey. August 7, 2012. http://pubs.usgs.gov/gip/dynamic/understanding.html#anchor6715825.

Le Treut, Hervé, Richard Somerville, Ulrich Cubasch, Yihui Ding, Cecilie Mauritzen, Abdalah Mokssit, Thomas Peterson, and Michael Prather. "Historical Overview of Climate Change Science." Intergovernmental Panel on Climate Change. 2007. Accessed June 28, 2014. https://www.ipcc.ch/pdf/assessment-report/ar4/wg1/ar4-wg1-chapter1.pdf.

"Timeline: 50 Years of Spaceflight." *Space.com.* September 28, 2012. http://www.space.com/4422-timeline-50-years-spaceflight.html.

Van Helden, Al. *The Galileo Project.* 1995. Accessed September 14, 2014. http://galileo.rice.edu/.

FURTHER INFORMATION

Gibson, Karen Bush. *Women in Space: 23 Stories of First Flights, Scientific Missions, and Gravity-Breaking Adventures.* Chicago: Chicago Review Press, 2014.
This book profiles twenty-three pioneers who became female astronauts, forging a path for other female astronauts and mission specialists to follow.

Miller, Ron. *Recentering the Universe: The Radical Theories of Copernicus, Kepler, Galileo, and Newton.* Minneapolis: Twenty-First Century Books, 2014.
Readers learn the exciting story of how scientists such as Copernicus, Kepler, Galileo, and Newton turned the structure of the universe inside out.

NASA Education
http://www.nasa.gov/audience/forstudents/5-8/index.html#.VDarHfldUbt
Check out this student-focused page to find out about NASA's upcoming and past missions and space technology, as well as exploring careers in space.

Silverstein, Alvin, Virginia Silverstein, and Laura Silverstein Nunn. *Plate Tectonics.* Minneapolis: Twenty-First Century Books, 2009.
The authors explain the theory of plate tectonics and how moving plates can cause some of the scariest natural disasters, such as earthquakes, volcanoes, and tsunamis. They also explore how plate tectonics are changing our planet and how they could affect our future on Earth.

Woodward, John. *Geography: A Visual Encyclopedia.* New York: DK, 2013. This full-color visual encyclopedia explores every aspect of our world, from the North Pole to the South Pole, from the outer atmosphere to the fiery core, and from natural processes to human impact.

INDEX

PHOTO ACKNOWLEDGMENTS

The images in this book are used with the permission of: NASA/Earth Science and Remote Sensing Unit, Johnson Space Center, pp. 5, 26 (bottom); © Ashmolean Museum, University of Oxford, UK/Bridgeman Images, pp. 6 (top left), 9; © Jerry Schad/Science Source, p. 6 (middle left); © Science Source, pp. 6 (bottom middle), 13 (right), 17 (bottom middle), 23 (left), 26 (right), 31; © AF Fotografie/Alamy, pp. 6 (bottom right); 10; © National Geographic Image Collection/Alamy, pp. 7 (left); 11 © Gianni Tortoli/Science Source, pp. 7 (bottom middle); 13 (left); © Private Collection/Bridgeman Images, pp. 7 (top middle), 26 (top left), 29; © Chistie's Images Ltd./SuperStock, p. 7 (right); © Sheila Terry/Science Source, p. 8; © Niday Picture Library/Alamy, p. 12; © iStockphoto.com/ Nancy Nehring, p. 15; © Pictoral Press Ltd/Alamy, pp. 16 (top left); 18; © RIA Novosti/ Science Source, p. 16 (bottom left); © Babak Tafreshi/Science Source, p. 16 (bottom right); © Photo Researchers/Alamy, pp. 16 (top right); 21 © NASA/Science Source, pp. 17 (left); 25; © Imagestate Media Partners Limited - ImpactPhotos/Alamy, pp. 17 (top middle); 23 (right) © Everett Collection Historial/Alamy, p. 17 (right); Brian Brondel/Wikimedia Commons (cc 3.0), p. 20; © Detlev van Ravenswaay/Science Source, p. 22; © Everett Collection Historial/Alamy, p. 24 (bottom); © Novosti Press Agency/Science Source, p. 24 (top); © Planetary Visions Ltd/Science Source, pp. 27 (left); 32; © W. Haxby, LDEO/ Science Source, p. 27 (bottom middle); © Gary Hincks/Science Source, p. 27 (top right); © Biblioteca Marciana, Venice, Italy/Giraudon/Bridgeman Images, p. 28; © LWM/NASA/ LANDSAT/Alamy, p. 30; © Encyclopaedia Britannica/UIG/Bridgeman Images, pp. 34 (top left), 36 (right), 40; © Monica Schroeder/Science Source, pp. 34 (middle left), 37; © Universal Images Group Limited/Alamy, p. 34 (bottom left); © G.S. Callendar Papers, University of East Anglia, p. 34 (bottom right); © Aqua Image/Alamy, p. 35 (bottom left); © iStockphoto.com/acilo, p. 35 (top left); AP Photo/Keystone/Salvatore Di Nolfi, p. 35 (bottom right); © Marco Longaria/AFP/Getty Images, p. 35 (top right); © Phil Degginger/ Alamy, p. 36 (left); © Photoconix/Alamy, p. 39; NASA/USGS, p. 41; © Marco Longaria/ AFP/Getty Images, p. 43; © iStockphoto.com/Cesare Ferarri (light burst).

Front cover: NASA/Johnson Space Center.